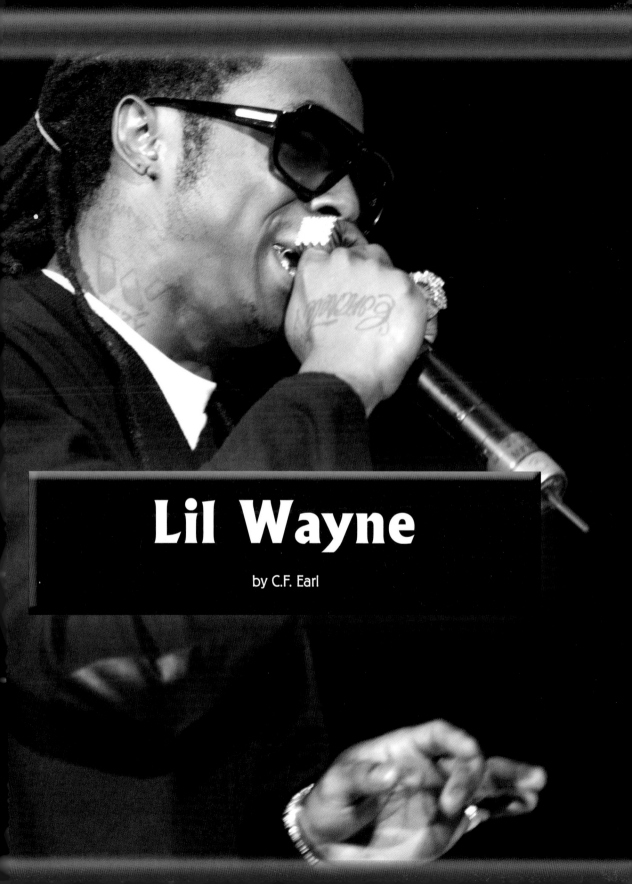

Lil Wayne

by C.F. Earl

Superstars of Hip-Hop

Lil Wayne

by C.F. Earl

Mason Crest

Lil Wayne

Mason Crest
370 Reed Road
Broomall, Pennsylvania 19008
www.masoncrest.com

Printed and bound in the United States of America.

First printing
9 8 7 6 5 4 3 2 1

Library of Congress Cataloging-in-Publication Data

Earl, C. F.
  Lil' Wayne / by C.F. Earl.
    p. cm. — (Superstars of hip hop)
  Includes index.
  ISBN 978-1-4222-2532-5 (hardcover) — ISBN 978-1-4222-2508-0 (series hardcover) — ISBN 978-1-4222-2558-5 (softcover) — ISBN 978-1-4222-9234-1 (ebook)
  1. Lil Wayne—Juvenile literature. 2. Rap musicians—United States—Biography—Juvenile literature. I. Title.
  ML3930.L49E27 2012
  782.421649092—dc22
  [B]
                        2011005809

Produced by Harding House Publishing Services, Inc.
www.hardinghousepages.com
Interior Design by MK Bassett-Harvey.
Cover design by Torque Advertising & Design.

Publisher's notes:
• All quotations in this book come from original sources and contain the spelling and grammatical inconsistencies of the original text.
• The Web sites mentioned in this book were active at the time of publication. The publisher is not responsible for Web sites that have changed their addresses or discontinued operation since the date of publication. The publisher will review and update the Web site addresses each time the book is reprinted.

DISCLAIMER: The following story has been thoroughly researched, and to the best of our knowledge, represents a true story. While every possible effort has been made to ensure accuracy, the publisher will not assume liability for damages caused by inaccuracies in the data, and makes no warranty on the accuracy of the information contained herein. This story has not been authorized nor endorsed by Lil Wayne.

Contents

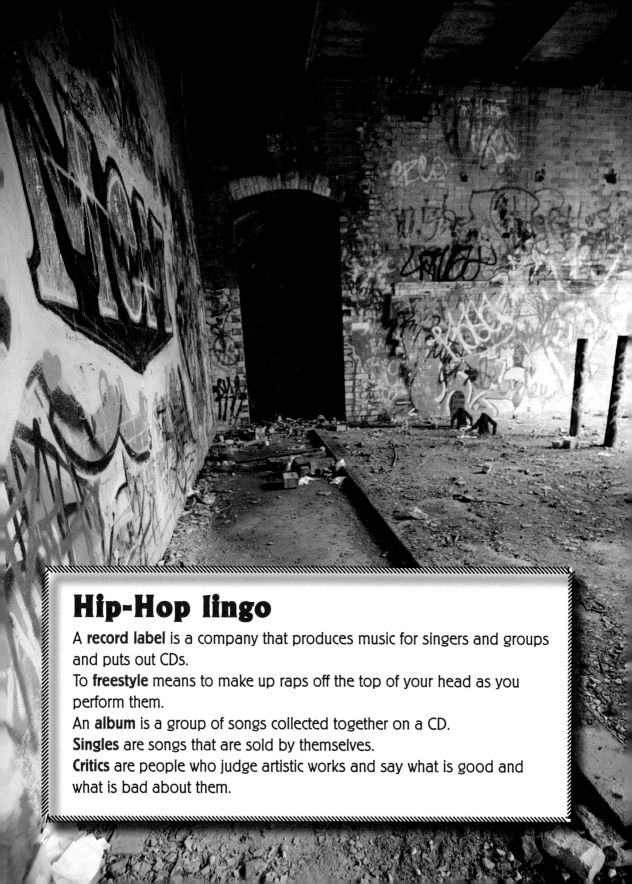

Hip-Hop lingo

A **record label** is a company that produces music for singers and groups and puts out CDs.

To **freestyle** means to make up raps off the top of your head as you perform them.

An **album** is a group of songs collected together on a CD.

Singles are songs that are sold by themselves.

Critics are people who judge artistic works and say what is good and what is bad about them.

Chapter 1

From Hollygrove to Hot Boys

Lil Wayne's real name is Dwayne Michael Carter, Jr. He was born on September 27, 1982, in New Orleans, Louisiana. His mother, Cita, was just nineteen when he was born. Dwayne didn't have any brothers and sisters. When he was two years old, his father left. Dwayne never really knew his father. For the first part of his life, Dwayne and Cita just had each other.

Dwayne and Cita lived in the Hollygrove neighborhood in New Orleans' 17th Ward. Life was hard in Hollygrove. Lots of families were poor. Lots of young people felt like they didn't have a chance in life. Some turned to selling drugs to make money.

In school, Dwayne was always a good student. He was smart and liked to succeed. At Lafayette Elementary, he was on the honor roll.

When Dwayne was twelve, he joined his middle school's drama club. He liked to perform for other people. He liked to have people watch him on-stage, even when he was young. He played the Tin Man in his school's performance of *The Wiz*, a musical.

Dwayne loved hip-hop more than anything. He loved performing, but he also loved words. Dwayne listened to the Geto Boys and lots of rappers from New Orleans.

Dwayne started rapping when he was only eight years old. He told an interviewer later that he rapped in a group called Kids With Attitude (K.W.A.). He said he'd rap on the porch of his house for anyone who would listen.

Baby Gangsta

Even though Dwayne was smart and did well in school, life was hard. At home, his mother started seeing a man named Reginald "Rabbit" Carter. Rabbit sold drugs to make money. Soon, he'd become Dwayne's stepfather.

Lil Wayne later said that that's when he learned about things he shouldn't have known about. He was around guns and drugs. He stopped focusing on school.

Around this time, Wayne went to an autograph signing by rapper Lil Slim. He was one of Dwayne's favorite rappers. At the signing, Dwayne met Brian "Baby" Williams—also known as Birdman—and Ronald "Slim" Williams. The brothers ran Cash Money Records together.

Dwayne told Baby that he rapped. Then Dwayne showed off his skills. When he was finished, Baby gave Dwayne his card. Now, Dwayne had Baby's phone number. And he was going to use it.

Cash Money was Dwayne's favorite **record label**. They had lots of artists Dwayne loved to listen to. Dwayne wanted to work for Cash Money more than any other label.

To get Baby's attention, Dwayne started to call the number on his card a lot. He'd call and leave messages. He **freestyled** verses into the phone. He wanted to prove to Baby he had what it took to be a rapper.

According to Lil Wayne, he could find all the trouble he wanted in school; it wasn't necessary for him to run the streets. And Lil Wayne did find trouble, becoming an excellent hustler.

Dwayne wasn't much older than ten. But Baby heard his talent in the phone messages. Baby knew Dwayne could be a great rapper. He decided that Cash Money Records should take a chance on Dwayne. So Baby signed Dwayne to the label.

When he was twelve, Dwayne started the rap group the B.G.'z with rapper B.G. B.G.'z stood for Baby Gangstaz. Dwayne used the name Baby D.

That same year, Dwayne accidentally shot himself. He was playing with a gun and it went off. The bullet nearly hit Dwayne's heart. It could have killed him, but he lived. The accident was a serious one, though.

Dwayne was starting his life in rap. But he was also taking risks. Playing with guns was a big risk!

In 1995, the B.G.'z put out *True Story*. The **album** had nine songs on it. Baby D rapped on three tracks. It was the start of Dwayne's rap career.

Dwayne was now more than a rap fan. He had already recorded an album. He was proving that he could succeed, no matter his age. And it was just the beginning for Dwayne Carter.

Hot Boys

Dwayne dropped out of high school when he was fourteen. He still did well in school, but he wanted to rap full time.

After *True Story*, Dwayne and B.G. joined rappers Juvenile and Turk. They formed the group Hot Boys. Dwayne started using the name Lil Wayne.

Lil Wayne told an interviewer later that he dropped the "D" from his name because of never knowing his father. His father's name was also Dwayne. He wanted to be different from his father.

Lil Wayne was the youngest member in Hot Boys. He was only fifteen. Wayne was going to have to grow up fast, though. Soon

When the Hot Boys released their first album, it was a hit—at least in the South. In the rest of the country, East and West coast artists, like Notorious B.I.G., Jay-Z, and Snoop Dogg (shown here), were still at the top of the hip-hop food chain.

after he joined Hot Boys, Wayne's first daughter was born. Now, Wayne was a father and needed to support a family. He needed to succeed in rap more than ever.

In 1997, Hot Boys released their first album. It was called *Get It How U Live!*

The album sold very well for a new rap group. *Get It How U Live!* sold around 400,000 copies. Most of the copies were sold in the South. The album sold best in New Orleans, home of the Hot Boys.

Dirty South rap is one of the biggest musical genres today.
And Lil Wayne is one of its biggest draws. He has a huge fan base who go to his concerts and buy his recordings.

Two years later, in 1999, Hot Boys released their second album. It was called *Guerrilla Warfare*. Lil Wayne was seventeen years old.

Guerrilla Warfare was the number-one hip-hop album in the country when it came out. It had two big **singles**, too. The first was called "We On Fire." The second was called "I Need A Hot Girl."

The album sold more than a million copies. Fans loved the album. **Critics** loved it, too.

In 2000, *The Source* magazine named Hot Boys the Group of the Year. Wayne had never had so much success. His life was going the way he wanted. He was becoming the rapper he had always wanted to be.

Hot Boys didn't last much longer, though. Soon, the group would split so each member could go out on his own.

Hip-Hop lingo

A **studio album** is a collection of songs put together in a recording studio.

The **singles chart** is a list of the best-selling songs for a week.

Chapter 2

Flying Solo

Just a few months after *Guerilla Warfare* came out, Lil Wayne was ready to put out his own album.

His first album came out on November 2, 1999. It was called *Tha Block Is Hot*. Cash Money Records released the album. Universal Records helped Cash Money get the album out. Cash Money and Universal had made a deal to do the same with all their albums.

The album had many guest verses from the Hot Boys. Juvenile, B.G., and Turk all helped on the album, too. Baby's Big Tymers also helped Wayne on the album.

The album was a big success for Wayne. It sold well and made it to number three on the album charts. It sold more than a million copies.

Tha Block Is Hot introduced Lil Wayne to many people who'd never heard of him. *The Source* magazine called Lil Wayne the Best New Rapper of 1999. Lil Wayne was now on his way to becoming one of rap's youngest successes.

Lil Wayne's next album came out a little more than a year after *Tha Block Is Hot*. It was called *Lights Out*.

Almost all of the guests on *Lights Out* were from Cash Money. Baby and the Hot Boys helped on *Lights Out*, just like they had on *Tha Block Is Hot*. *Lights Out* had fewer guest verses, though. The album was much more Wayne's than it was the Hot Boys'.

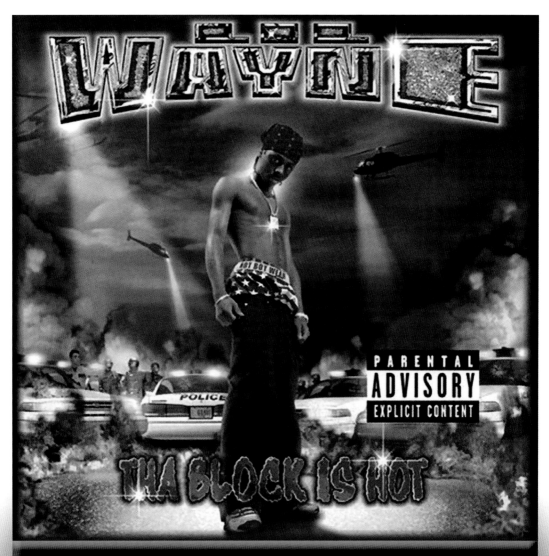

It would only be a matter of time before Lil Wayne hit it big. With albums and mixtapes, Lil Wayne climbed his way up the charts and saw his fan base grow. But there were bumps—sometimes big ones—along the climb.

The Hot Boys weren't getting along very well. Juvenile, B.G., and Turk said they weren't happy with how Cash Money Records was handling their payments. They thought Lil Wayne was getting more attention (and money) from the company. The Hot Boys soon split up. Juvenile, B.G., and Turk left Cash Money. By the time *Lights Out* came out in December 2000, Lil Wayne was the last of the Hot Boys left.

Lights Out wasn't as successful as *Tha Block Is Hot*. The album didn't sell as well as Wayne's first album. It only sold around half a million copies.

In 2002, Wayne released his third album. This one was called *500 Degreez*. The album came out on July 23. Like *Lights Out*, the album didn't sell as well as *Tha Block Is Hot*.

Tha Carter

After two albums that didn't sell as well as his first, some people thought Lil Wayne might be done. But Lil Wayne wanted to prove those people wrong. He was ready to be rap's next big thing. He wasn't even close to being done.

In June 2004, Wayne released *Tha Carter*. It was his fourth **studio album**. Many fans believe *Tha Carter* is when Lil Wayne started to show his true skills.

"Go DJ" was the first single from *Tha Carter*. It became a hit for Wayne. It moved quickly up the **singles chart** to be in the top five. With the success of "Go DJ," *Tha Carter* sold even more.

Tha Carter was a huge success for Wayne. The album sold more than a million copies. It also brought Wayne new fans and got more people interested in his music.

Wayne had started rapping almost ten years earlier. Now, he was gaining the success he really wanted. Lil Wayne was ready to become the star he always knew he could be.

Everyone in New Orleans knew that Hurricane Katrina was on its way and that they should leave. After all, the city sits below sea level. But, if you don't have a car or access to public transportation, how are you supposed to evacuate?

New Orleans and Katrina

On August 25, 2005, Hurricane Katrina hit the coast of Louisiana. New Orleans was hit very hard by the storm. Levees—great walls made to keep the city from flooding—broke down. Water entered neighborhood after neighborhood.

Many people couldn't get out ahead of the storm. They stayed in their homes until they were flooded. Some people escaped to the roofs of their houses. They waited for help, but it was slow in

Lil Wayne's neighborhood was hit hard by Hurricane Katrina in 2005. Though his 17th Ward neighborhood had been filled with crime and poverty when he was growing up, it had still been his home and an important part of who he is.

coming. Many people died because of Hurricane Katrina. In New Orleans and many other Southern cities, the storm did a lot of damage.

Hurricane Katrina was one of the worst natural disasters in the history of the United States. More than 80 percent of New Orleans was underwater. More than 1,800 people died. Hurricane Katrina was a huge tragedy for the people of New Orleans. Their city just wasn't the same. Lots of people needed help. It was hard to see their home hurt by the storm.

Many people in New Orleans were angry. Why hadn't the government been more ready for the storm? Why didn't help come right away? Why didn't the levees hold up and keep the water out of the city?

Lil Wayne's neighborhood was hit hard by the storm. The 17th Ward was one of the places where a levee broke. Lil Wayne's neighborhood was flooded.

The storm was personal for Wayne. He was mad, just like many people in New Orleans. New Orleans was his home. It was also the home of Cash Money Records.

To deal with the tragedy, Wayne went back to making music. It had always helped him through hard times before. Making his next album was also a way to help his New Orleans fans have something to hold on to. Wayne donated money to build a park in his old neighborhood. The storm hurt New Orleans, but Wayne wanted to show that it hadn't finished the city.

Tha Carter II

On December 6, 2005, Lil Wayne put out *Tha Carter II*. The album was the follow-up to Wayne's *Tha Carter*.

Tha Carter II sold more than 235,000 copies in its first week out. It was the fastest any Lil Wayne album had sold. *Tha Carter II* was the number-two album in the country the week it came out.

When Lil Wayne released *Tha Carter*, there was no doubt that he was meant to be a star. Everyone seemed to love the young artist's sound. He worked hard, and it paid off.

Mannie Fresh was one of the best producers at Cash Money. Many gave him much of the credit for Lil Wayne's success. When Mannie decided to move on, some wondered whether Lil Wayne's career would survive.

Tha Carter II was the first Lil Wayne album that wasn't produced by Mannie Fresh. Fresh was part of Baby's Big Tymers. He produced all of Cash Money's albums between 1993 and 2005. After that, he left Cash Money Records.

Tha Carter II had three singles. The first was called "Fireman." The song was Lil Wayne's biggest hit since "Go DJ." The next single was called "Hustler Musik." The third single from *Tha Carter II* was called "Shooter." The song featured R&B singer Robin Thicke.

Tha Carter II was a huge success for Wayne. The album has sold more than two million copies since it came out. It brought Wayne new fans and was a hit with critics, too.

Tha Carter II is also the point when Lil Wayne started calling himself the best rapper alive. He even named a song "Best Rapper Alive." It's a boast that Wayne is known for. His fans believe it's true. His critics say he's just a young rapper trying to make a name for himself. No matter what people said, though, Wayne didn't let the talk slow him down. He just wanted to prove he was the best.

Hip-Hop lingo

Mixtapes are collections of a few songs put on a CD or given away for free on the Internet without being professionally recorded.

An **imprint** is a company that is organized as part of another company, with a different name.

When someone is **headlining** a show, he is the main performer.

When a person is **sentenced** in court, a judge tells him what the punishment for his crime will be.

To **express** yourself means to show what you are thinking or feeling.

The **charts** are lists of the best-selling songs and albums for a week.

Each year, the National Academy of Recording Arts and Sciences gives out the **Grammy Awards** (short for Gramophone Awards)—or Grammys—to people who have done something really big in the music industry.

A **tribute** is something created to let people know how much a person, place, or thing is appreciated.

Consequences are what happens because of something a person has said or done.

Chapter 3

The Best Rapper Alive

Lil Wayne didn't slow down after *Tha Carter II*. He just kept recording new music.

Wayne didn't record like other artists. Many rappers will record a couple times a year. Wayne recorded all the time. He carried a microphone and recording equipment with him wherever he traveled.

Lil Wayne is known for not writing his rhymes down. Instead, he just records them right away. It's a way of always having new music for fans. It's also a way for Wayne to get things off his chest. He says that recording his ideas lets him think about other things.

Mixtapes have always been a part of hip-hop. In the past, they were sometimes handed out for free on the street. Today, they are passed around on the Internet. Many mixtapes are given out as free downloads online.

Mixtapes are a way for rappers to stay in people's minds when they aren't on the TV or radio. They're a way to make sure fans have new music, even if they don't have a new album to listen to.

Lil Wayne records so much that he's able to put out many mixtapes. After *Tha Carter II*, Wayne started putting out lots of mixtapes.

He worked on an album called *Like Father, Like Son* with Birdman (Baby's new name). The album made it to number three on the album charts. It sold well and was another big success.

Wayne also worked with DJ Drama to create several mixtapes called *Dedication*. The first *Dedication* mixtape came out before *Tha Carter II*. *Dedication 2* came out in 2006. Wayne would work with DJ Drama later on a third *Dedication* mixtape, too.

Dedication 2 featured the song "Georgia . . . Bush." In the song, Lil Wayne raps about Hurricane Katrina. His verses talk about how President Bush failed New Orleans after the storm. The song shows how much New Orleans means to Wayne. It also shows how he feels about Hurricane Katrina.

Lil Wayne also released a series of mixtapes called *Da Drought*. In 2007, *Da Drought 3* got lots of attention. Many people believe the album showed a better Lil Wayne. They said it showed a lot of change in Wayne's flow and lyrics.

In 2007 and 2008, Lil Wayne worked on his next studio album. But some tracks were leaked onto the Internet. Some fans put out unofficial mixtapes. They were called *The Drought Is Over*. They featured some of the songs from Lil Wayne's next album.

Instead of keeping the leaked songs on his next album, Wayne started over. He began recording new songs for the album. He might have been mad about his songs leaking, but he never showed it. He just kept making more music.

In 2008, he released a small album called *The Leak*. *The Leak* was a bit like a short mixtape. It had some songs that were recorded for his next album. He put it out before the album so fans could have something to look forward to.

Lots of people think that Lil Wayne's mixtapes show him at his best. They have helped him gain more fans. The mixtapes have let people know to look for his new albums. Mixtapes have been a big part of Lil Wayne's success. Even the mixtapes he didn't put out himself have kept Lil Wayne on fans' minds.

Young Money

In 2005, after *Tha Carter II* came out, Lil Wayne started Young Money Entertainment. Young Money was going to be Wayne's own label. It was an **imprint** of Cash Money Records. Wayne was going to help decide who was signed to Young Money. He would also help plan out the albums that Young Money artists' released.

In 2007, Lil Wayne was named president of Cash Money Records. He was also made the CEO of Young Money Entertainment. Later that year, though, Wayne gave up running the two companies. His manager and friend from childhood Cortez Bryant took over.

Young Money showed how far Cash Money had come since Lil Wayne started rapping. Wayne, Baby, and others had helped make Cash Money a label that people looked up to.

Lil Wayne was becoming the label's biggest star, too. And he was just 23 years old.

No Role Model

It seemed Lil Wayne's life couldn't get any better. He was successful in the rap game. His music was gaining him fans and album sales. Wayne's life was about to take a turn for the worse, though.

On July 23, 2007, Lil Wayne was **headlining** his first concert in New York City. The show was a huge success for Wayne. He'd made it further than most rappers ever dreamed of. But it wasn't going to be a good night for Lil Wayne.

Trouble seems to follow certain hip-hop artists until some are better known for their legal problems than for their music. Lil Wayne seemed to escape the reputation as a trouble-making artist. In 2007, however, he was arrested after a New York City concert.

After the show, New York City Police arrested Lil Wayne. They said he was using drugs. They also said he had a gun without a license. After a long trial, Wayne pled guilty to having the gun illegally. Wayne was **sentenced** to a year in prison. He had to start the year in March of 2010.

It was a low moment for Lil Wayne. But at the time, 2010 was a long time away. So Wayne got back to making music.

Wayne makes no secret about the fact that he's done bad things. What Wayne has said is that he's no role model. He doesn't rap to teach people to be good. He raps to **express** himself.

Tha Carter III

On June 10, 2008, Lil Wayne put out his sixth album. The album was called *Tha Carter III*.

Tha Carter III came out after Wayne had put out many mixtapes. He had also been rapping guest verses on many other artists' songs. More people knew about Lil Wayne than ever before. So when *Tha Carter III* came out, lots of people knew about the album.

Tha Carter III was a huge hit. In the first week the album was out, it sold more than one million copies. By the end of 2008, the album had sold around 2.88 million copies. The album has now sold more than three and a half million copies.

The album had a few successful singles. The first was called "Lollipop." It's still Wayne's biggest hit song. "Lollipop" became the number-one song in the country on the **charts**. *Tha Carter III* also featured "A Milli," "Got Money," and "Mrs. Officer."

Tha Carter III had many guest artists and producers. The album features verses from Jay-Z, Juelz Santana, Fabolous, Busta Rhymes, and others. T-Pain, Babyface, Bobby Valentino, and Robin Thicke

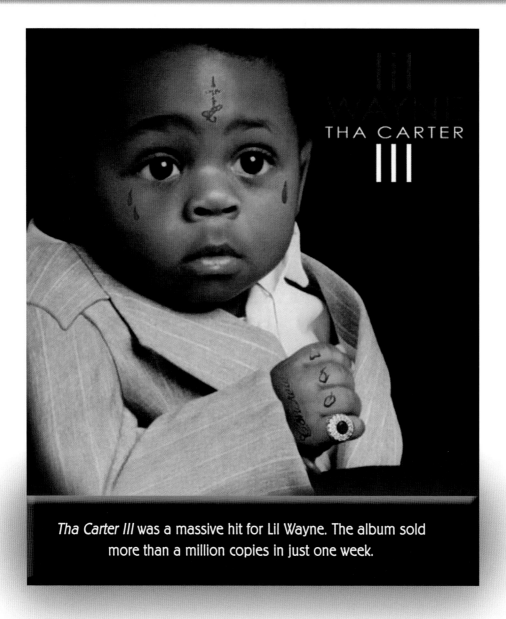

Tha Carter III was a massive hit for Lil Wayne. The album sold more than a million copies in just one week.

all sang on the album. Kanye West, The Alchemist, David Banner, Swizz Beatz, and other producers all made beats for it.

At the 51st **Grammy Awards** in 2009, Lil Wayne won Best Rap Album for *Tha Carter III*. Wayne also won Grammys for Best Rap Song (for "Lollipop") and Best Rap Performance (for "A Milli").

Lil Wayne performed twice at the award show. First, he performed "Swagga Like Us" with T.I., Kanye West, Jay-Z, and M.I.A. Then, Wayne and Robin Thicke performed "Tie My Hands" from *Tha Carter III*. The song is a **tribute** to Wayne's hometown of New Orleans. During the performance, video of New Orleans after Hurricane Katrina played behind Wayne and Thicke.

Lil Wayne's final line in his performance of "Tie My Hands" was "In every cloud there is a silver lining." With *Tha Carter III*, Wayne had reached a new level. He'd seen his city underwater. He'd been arrested and faced the **consequences** of his actions. But now, Lil Wayne was on top of the world.

Hip-Hop lingo

A **mentor** is a person who teaches someone else life lessons.

Chapter 4

Jail Time for Lil Wayne

After *Tha Carter III*, Wayne was doing great. His album had sold more in one week than most rappers' albums sell in their whole lives.

It was time for Wayne to start growing his Young Money crew. People were interested to see what was going to come next from Cash Money Records, too. Cash Money had made Lil Wayne into one of rap's biggest stars. Could it do the same with another artist?

In 2009, Canadian rapper Drake signed with Young Money and Cash Money. The new rapper released *So Far Gone* in September 2009. The short album was based on a mixtape Drake released the same year.

In 2010, Drake released his first full album. It was called *Thank Me Later*. The album was a huge success. With it, Drake became one of the biggest rappers of 2010. After Wayne went to jail, Drake became one of the most popular members of Young Money. Drake's 2011 album *Take Care* was one of the best-selling rap albums of the year.

Drake has said that Lil Wayne is his **mentor**. The two have worked on lots of songs together since Drake joined Young Money. Wayne and Drake have even talked about making a whole album together.

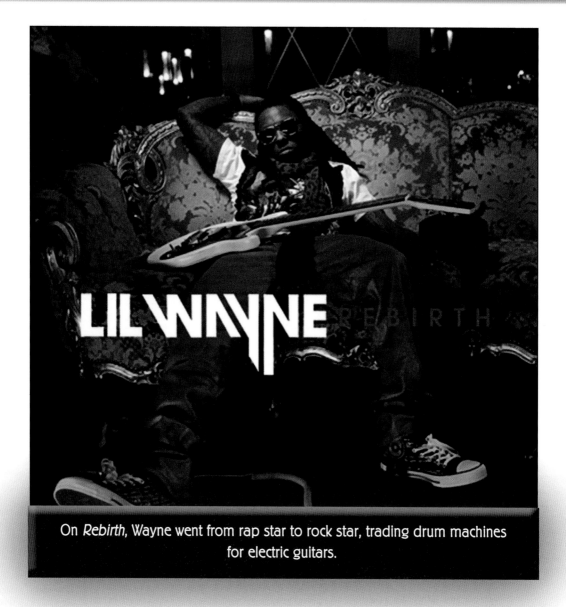

On *Rebirth*, Wayne went from rap star to rock star, trading drum machines for electric guitars.

In August 2009, Young Money signed rapper Nicki Minaj. She was making lots of popular mixtapes at the time. She had also won awards in a few magazines, even without an album or record deal. Lil Wayne and Young Money saw that Nicki could be a star. Her music and shows were fun. She fit right in with Young Money.

Nicki's first full album was released on November 22, 2010. It was called *Pink Friday*. The album was number two in the country the week it came out. *Pink Friday* sold more than 400,000 copies in its first week.

In the years after *Tha Carter III*, Young Money grew to be one of rap's most important labels. Today, the label is home to many rappers.

On December 21, 2009, Young Money put out *We Are Young Money*. The album was a group of songs by different Young Money artists. Almost every song featured Lil Wayne. The album featured Young Money artists like Jae Mills, Gudda Gudda, Gucci Mane, Tyga, and Mack Maine.

We Are Young Money was meant to show new Young Money artists to the world. Wayne has said that Young Money is also hard at work on getting albums out for these newer artists. Young Money and Cash Money are very important to Wayne. He has said that he feels like they are his family.

Lil Wayne and Birdman have grown close since Wayne started at Cash Money. Wayne calls Birdman his father. Wayne calls himself Birdman Jr. on many songs. Birdman has said that he basically adopted Wayne after his stepfather passed away. That was around the time Wayne joined Cash Money. The two have been growing closer ever since. Today, they say they are like father and son.

Rebirth

Lil Wayne released his next album on February 10, 2010. It was called *Rebirth*. Wayne told fans that *Rebirth* was his first rock album.

The beats on *Rebirth* were based on guitars as much as drums. Wayne wanted to be a rock star. He'd played guitar before, but he wanted to take it to the next level. *Rebirth* was his shot at being a true rock star.

At first, *Rebirth* was supposed to be released much earlier. Wayne had told fans he wanted to released *Tha Carter III* again with

Rebirth as a second disc. Instead, the album kept getting pushed back. After a while, he decided it was going to be its own album.

Before *Rebirth* came out, Wayne put out a few singles from the album. The first was called "Prom Queen." The hard rock beat was a new sound for Lil Wayne. The next single was called "On Fire."

After the album came out, Wayne put out "Drop the World" as a single. The song features Eminem rapping the second verse.

Rebirth wasn't as popular as *Tha Carter III.* It sold well, but many fans didn't like Wayne's take on rock music. They wanted the Best Rapper Alive to make rap, not rock.

Wayne's never been worried about what other people think, though. He wanted to make a rock record, so he did.

Rebirth was Wayne just being himself. He told fans that the album might sound different, but he was still the same artist he'd always been. He said he was just trying new things and doing what came to him.

Jail Time for Lil Wayne

Rebirth was the last Lil Wayne album released before the rapper went to jail for his 2007 arrest.

In the months before Wayne went to jail, he recorded all the time. He wanted to make sure he had enough new music for his fans to listen to while he was away. Wayne's sentence was only a year, but Wayne knew it could feel like a long time for fans.

In March 2010, Lil Wayne started serving his sentence at Riker's Island in New York.

Wayne wanted to keep in touch with his fans while he was gone. So, he had his friends set up a website. They called the site WeezyThnxYou.com. Wayne would write letters to his fans from jail, and the website would post them.

In his letters, Wayne talked about living in jail. He said he worked out and read a lot. He also wrote about getting letters from fans. Wayne would read the letters and write back to his fans. Sometimes he'd respond on WeezyThnxYou.com. Wayne said that the letters from fans helped him to understand how much his music meant to people. He said he was very thankful for the support.

Wayne had to wait for his sentence to end at Riker's. A year could be a long time. In music, an artist that is popular this year might not be popular next year. Wayne knew he needed to keep his name on people's minds. With WeezyThnxYou.com, he'd found one way. But as an artist, he had another idea as well.

I Am Not a Human Being

On September 27, 2010, Lil Wayne released *I Am Not a Human Being*. The album was put out on Wayne's birthday. It was also released while he was still in jail.

I Am Not a Human Being had ten songs on it. The songs were recorded before Lil Wayne went to jail, so that it could be released while he was inside. At first, Wayne wanted to put the songs from *I Am Not a Human Being* on a different album. He was working on songs for *Tha Carter IV* but decided they would be better on *I Am Not a Human Being*.

The album featured many artists from Wayne's Young Money crew. Drake shows up on four songs on the album. Nicki Minaj sings the hook on the song "What's Wrong With Them."

The album sold 250,000 copies in one month. "Right Above It" was a successful single, too. The song features Drake rapping the opening verse.

I Am Not a Human Being moved to number one on the album charts on October 20, 2010. It was the first time since Tupac Shakur died that an artist had a number-one album while in jail.

Freed Weezy

On November 4, 2010, Lil Wayne was released from Riker's Island. He'd served eight months in jail. Lil Wayne was released earlier than his year sentence because of good behavior.

During his time in jail, lots of new verses and new songs were coming out. Wayne had done enough work before going to jail that it felt like he never left music. Fans could still hear Wayne all over the place. He stayed close to the fans with his letters, too.

A few days before Wayne left jail, former President Bill Clinton had some words for the rapper. Clinton told a radio interviewer that his daughter had shown him hip-hop music. He said he thought Lil Wayne was very smart. He said Wayne had real ability.

The former President also said he hoped Wayne would have a good life after jail. Clinton said Wayne had been given another chance.

On November 6, 2010, Lil Wayne surprised fans by showing up at a Drake concert in Las Vegas. Wayne rapped his verse from Drake's song "Miss Me." Wayne ended his performance by telling fans "I'm back." And the fans couldn't have been happier to have him out of jail!

Tha Carter IV

After leaving prison at the end of 2010, Lil Wayne was ready to get back to music. He started work on his next album right away. Wayne had been promising to release *Tha Carter IV* for years. Now, he was going to make good on that promise.

The first single from *Tha Carter IV* came out in December 2010. The song was called "6 Foot, 7 Foot." Cash Money rapper Cory Gunz rapped with Wayne on the song. "6 Foot, 7 Foot" let fans know what to expect from Lil Wayne's next album.

After "6 Foot, 7 Foot," Lil Wayne put out a song called "John" with rapper Rick Ross. Next, Wayne put out a slow song called "How to Love." Instead of rapping, Wayne sang on the love song. He said he was inspired by songs he listened to on the radio in prison. "How to Love" was a big hit for Wayne. The song was on the radio a lot and many people who'd never heard Lil Wayne's music before heard him for the first time listening to "How to Love." The song showed Wayne's biggest fans a different side of their favorite rapper.

Tha Carter IV came out on August 29, 2011. The album was a huge success. In its first week out, *Tha Carter IV* sold almost one million copies. The album hit number-one on the *Billboard* album charts, too. Just like *Tha Carter III* before it, *Tha Carter IV* was one of the biggest rap records of the year. Lil Wayne was still on top of the rap world.

Lil Wayne's busy with more than his own music, too. He's helped make superstars of rappers Drake and Nicki Minaj. He's working with new artists on Cash Money and helping to make the record label one of the biggest in music.

After years in the game, Lil Wayne is still one of the most successful artists in rap. He's always working on new music for his huge number of fans around the world. No matter what Lil Wayne does next, he'll be working hard to prove that he really is the best rapper alive.

1970s Hip-hop is born in the Bronx section of New York City.

1979 "Rapper's Delight," by the Sugarhill Gang is released, the first hip-hop record to achieve mainstream success.

September 27, 1982
Dwayne Michael Carter, Jr., Lil Wayne, is born in New Orleans, Louisiana.

1988 It Takes a *Nation of Millions to Hold Us Back* by Public Enemy is released, considered by many to be one of hip-hop's most influential albums.

1990s Gangsta rap makes it big.

1995 Twelve-year-old Lil Wayne records his first singles for B.G.'s debut album.

1997 Lil Wayne's group Hot Boys releases its first album, *Get It How U Live!*

1999 Hot Boys' *Guerrilla Warfare* hits the top of the music charts.

November 1999
Lil Wayne releases his solo debut album.

2000 The Hot Boys are named Group of the Year by *Source* magazine.

2000 Lil Wayne is nominated for the Source Award for Best New Artist of the Year, Solo.

2000 Lil Wayne stars in his first movie, *Baller Blockin.*

2000 Hot Boys break up.

December 5, 2000
Lil Wayne releases his second solo album.

Early 2000s Dirty South rap takes over the hip-hop music scene.

August 2005
Hurricane Katrina devastates New Orleans; Lil Wayne participates in many relief efforts.

2007 Lil Wayne stars in *Who's Your Caddy?*

2007 Lil Wayne and Birdman win the BET Viewer's Choice Award for Best Video.

July 23, 2007
Lil Wayne is arrested for possession of a pistol and smoking marijuana near a tour bus.

October 5, 2007
He is arrested again for an outstanding felony drug possession charge.

January 2008
Lil Wayne is arrested on felony drug charges.

2008 Lil Wayne stars in *Cut Throat City*.

2008 A duo is formed with T-Pain; they call it T-Wayne.

2009 Lil Wayne releases *No Ceilings*.

October 22, 2009
Lil Wayne pleads guilty to attempted criminal possession of a weapon.

October 2009
Lil Wayne gets sued for $1.4 million for copyright infringement.

March 8, 2010
Lil Wayne is sentenced to a year in prison in Rikers Island.

September, 2010

> Lil Wayne releases *I Am Not a Human Being.*

November, 2010

> Lil Wayne is released from prison.

2011   Lil Wayne releases *Tha Carter IV.*

Discography

Albums

1999	Tha Block Is Hot
2000	Lights Out
2002	500 Degrees
2004	Tha Carter
2005	Tha Carter II
2008	Tha Carter III
2010	Rebirth
	I Am Not a Human Being
2011	Tha Carter IV

Films

2000	Baller Blockin
2007	Who's Your Caddy?
2009	Tha Carter Documentary
2010	Hurricane Season

Books

Baker, Soren. *The History of Rap and Hip Hop*. San Diego, Calif.: Lucent, 2006.

Comissiong, Solomon W. F. *How Jamal Discovered Hip-Hop Culture*. New York: Xlibris, 2008.

Cornish, Melanie. *The History of Hip Hop*. New York: Crabtree, 2009.

Czekaj, Jef. *Hip and Hop, Don't Stop!* New York: Hyperion, 2010.

Haskins, Jim. *One Nation Under a Groove: Rap Music and Its Roots*. New York: Jump at the Sun, 2000.

Hatch, Thomas. *A History of Hip-Hop: The Roots of Rap*. Portsmouth, N.H.: Red Bricklearning, 2005.

Websites

Cash Money Records
www.cashmoney-records.com

Lil Wayne Official Site
www.lilwayne-online.com

Lil Wayne on MTV
www.mtv.com/music/artist/lil_wayne/artist.jhtml

Lil Wayne on MySpace
www.myspace.com/lilwayne

Lil Wayne on VH1
www.vh1.com/artists/az/lil_wayne/artist.jhtml

Index

About the Author

C.F. Earl is a writer living and working in Binghamton, New York. Earl writes mostly on social and historical topics, including health, the military, and finances. An avid student of the world around him, and particularly fascinated with almost any current issue, C.F. Earl hopes to continue to write for books, websites, and other publications for as long as he is able.

Picture Credits

iStock: p. 18, 28
> Gingerich, Andrea: p. 6
> Glade, Christine: p. 9
> McClunie, Nathan: p. 12
> Schnieder, Doug: p. 19

PR Photos
> Bielawski, Adam: p. 1, 14, 21, 24
> Garces, Juan: p. 22
> Hatcher, Chris: p. 11

Universal Records/Cash Money Records: pp. 16, 30, 34

To the best knowledge of the publisher, all other images are in the public domain. If any image has been inadvertently uncredited, please notify Harding House Publishing Services, Vestal, New York 13850, so that rectification can be made for future printings.